TIME TRAVEL GUIDES

THE RENAISSANCE

Anna Claybourne

Chicago, Illinois

© 2008 Raintree
Published by Raintree,
a division of Reed Elsevier Inc.
Chicago, Illinois

Customer Service 888–454–2279

Visit our website at www.heinemannraintree.com

Designed by Clare Nicholas
Illustrations by Peter Bull
Printed and bound in China by Leo
    Paper Group

12 11 10 09 08
10 9 8 7 6 5 4 3 2 1

Library of Congress Cataloging-in-Publication Data
Claybourne, Anna.
  The Renaissance / Anna Claybourne.
    p. cm. – (Time travel guides)
  Includes bibliographical references and index.
  ISBN 978-1-4109-2910-5 (library binding, hardcover)
  – ISBN 978-1-4109-2916-7 (pbk.)
  1. Renaissance–Juvenile literature. 2. Europe–History-
-476-1492–Juvenile literature. 3. Europe–History–
1492-1648–Juvenile literature. 4. Europe–Social life and
customs–Juvenile literature. I. Title.

CB361.C54 2008
940.2'1–dc22

                          2007006027

Acknowledgments
The publishers would like to thank the following for permission to reproduce photographs:
AKG p. **46**; Art Archive pp. **17** (Musée de Louvre, Paris/ Dagli Orti), **19** (Dagli Orti), **23** (Art Archive), **24** (Manoir du Clos Lucé/Dagli Orti), **25** (Bibliothèque des Arts Décoratifs/Dagli Orti), **29** (National Gallery, London/ Eileen Tweedy), **32** (Château de Beauregard, Val de Loire/ Dagli Orti), **34** (Monte dei Paschi Bank, Siena/Dagli Orti), **42** (Bibliothèque des Arts Décoratifs/Dagli Orti), **44** (Museo Civico Cremona/Dagli Orti), **45** (Palazzo Barberini, Rome/Dagli Orti), **47** (Art Archive), **48–49** (Château de Blois/Dagli Orti) **52** (Castello di Issogne, Val d'Aosta, Italy/Dagli Orti), **53** (Biblioteca Nazionale, Marciana, Venice/Dagli Orti); Brand X Pictures pp. **10**, **12–13**; Bridgeman Art Library pp. **8** (The Stapleton Collection), **11** (Palazzo Medici-Riccardi, Florence), **14** (British Library, London), **15** (Santa Maria Novella, Florence), **18** (Palazzo Ducale, Mantua), **21** (Victoria & Albert Museum, London), **33** (Château de Versailles, France/Lauros/Giraudon), **35** (Museum Narodowe, Poznan, Poland), **36** (Castello di Issogne, Val d'Aosta, Italy/Giraudon), **38** (Christie's Images), **39** (British Museum, London), **40–41** (Galleria dell' Accademia, Venice), **51** (Giraudon), **54–55** (Galleria degli Uffizi, Florence); Corbis pp. **6–7** (Carl & Ann Purcell), **26–27** (Guenter Rossenbach/zefa), **28** (Gregor Schuster/zefa), **30** (Nik Wheeler); iStockphoto p. **22** (Ogen Perry).

Background cover photograph of Florence Cathedral reproduced with permission of Brand X Pictures. Inset photographs of map and brass globe reproduced with permission of AKG-images.

The publishers would like to thank Professor Norman Tanner for his assistance in the preparation of this book.

Every effort has been made to contact copyright holders of any material reproduced in this book. Any omissions will be rectified in subsequent printings if notice is given to the publishers.

Disclaimer
All the Internet addresses (URLs) given in this book were valid at the time of going to press. However, due to the dynamic nature of the Internet, some addresses may have changed, or sites may have changed or ceased to exist since publication. While the author and publishers regret any inconvenience this may cause readers, no responsibility for any such changes can be accepted by either the author or the publishers.

CONTENTS

Map of Renaissance Europe in About 1500   4

Chapter 1: Facts About the Renaissance   6

Chapter 2: Everyday Life   12

Chapter 3: Things to See and Do   26

Chapter 4: On the Move   40

Chapter 5: If Things Go Wrong   48

Chapter 6: Useful Information   54

Further Reading   *61*

Glossary   *62*

Index   *64*

Words that appear in the text in bold, **like this**, are explained in the glossary.

ATLANTIC

OCEAN

SCOTLAND
IRELAND

Globe
Theater

MAP OF RENAISSANCE EUROPE IN ABOUT 1500

WALES

ENGLAND

London

Paris

The Louvre

FRANCE

Santiago de
Compostela

NAVARRE

PORTUGAL

Lisbon

Madrid

Barcelona

SPAIN

Tangier

MEDITERRANEAN SEA

ALGIERS

NORWAY

NORTH
SEA

SWEDEN

TEUTONIC
ORDER

MUSCOVY

DENMARK

TEUTONIC
ORDER

HOLY
ROMAN
EMPIRE

POLAND

N

W   E

S

LITHUANIA

RHINE

BOHEMIA

Vienna

SAVOY

AUSTRIA

HUNGARY

MOLDAVIA

Milan

VENETIAN REPUBLIC

Venice

DANUBE

Genoa

Bologna

WALLACHIA

Florence

PAPAL
STATES

Rome

KINGDOM
OF
NAPLES

Constantinople (Istanbul)

OTTOMAN

St. Peter's Basilica

EMPIRE

This modern view of Venice, in Italy, would have looked very similar in Renaissance times.

CHAPTER 1

FACTS ABOUT THE RENAISSANCE

A time traveler in Europe could hardly visit a more important era than the Renaissance. Turn back the clock 500 years, and you can explore a time when art, fashion, and music entered a new age, inventors were bursting with ideas, and European explorers were discovering the rest of the globe. The Renaissance sowed the seeds of the modern world. Open the first books printed on a printing press, look through the first telescope, and meet great geniuses such as da Vinci, Michelangelo, and Shakespeare. Italy leads the Renaissance and is home to many of its greatest artists, scientists, and inventors, so it is definitely the best place to start your journey.

WHEN TO VISIT

The Renaissance (French for "rebirth") is a boom in ideas, art, and culture. The Renaissance period begins in the early 1400s, in Italy, and lasts between 200 and 300 years, depending on where you are in Europe (it reaches the northern countries later and lasts longer there). It develops from an earlier era known as the **medieval** period. It is best to visit in the late 1400s, when the Renaissance is at its peak in Italy.

CAUSES OF THE RENAISSANCE

- Trade: Transportation around the world is improving, and more people are getting rich through trade. They now have money to spend on fashion and the arts.
- Books: Thanks to the invention of the printing press in the 1450s, books can be printed quickly and ideas can spread fast.
- **Classical** times: People are rediscovering the Classical age—that is, ancient Greece and Rome. Classical art and literature inspire Renaissance writers and artists.
- The fall of Constantinople: In 1453 the great city of Constantinople (in what is now Turkey) is taken over from the Greeks by the Ottoman Empire. Many Greek scholars flee to European lands, such as Italy, taking their skills and ideas with them.

This engraving, made in about 1600, shows ➞ Renaissance printers arranging type into pages and operating printing machines.

- Cities: New jobs and the promise of wealth are drawing people to the cities. Bigger cities enable more people to meet up, share ideas, design buildings, hold concerts, and set up universities.
- **Humanism**: *Humanism* means an understanding of the world based on human experiences, ideas, and thoughts. For many writers and thinkers in the Renaissance, this is gradually becoming more important than older ideas based on religious teachings and rules.

GOOD AND BAD TIMES TO VISIT

1304–1374	Life of Italian writer Francesco Petrarch, "father of the Renaissance."
1346–1351	The Black Death (a horrible plague) strikes northern Europe.
1420	Portugese prince Henry the Navigator sends sailors to explore the coast of Africa.
1430s	Invention of printing press.
1436	Florence cathedral's dome designed by Italian Filippo Brunelleschi.
1452	Leonardo da Vinci born near Florence, in Italy.
1469–1492	Italian Lorenzo de' Medici controls Florence and pays for many works of art.
1492	Italian explorer Christopher Columbus discovers the Americas.
1503–1506	Italian artist Leonardo da Vinci paints his most famous painting, the *Mona Lisa*.
1509–1547	King Henry VIII, a major **patron** of the arts, reigns in England.
1512	Italian artist Michelangelo finishes painting Rome's Sistine Chapel.
1543	Polish astronomer Nicolaus Copernicus publishes his theory that Earth moves around the Sun.
1564	Birth of the great English writer William Shakespeare.
1618–1648	Thirty Years' War.

Key:

Stay away   Interesting times to visit   Best times to visit

WHERE TO GO

If you are heading for Renaissance Europe in the late 1400s, your main destination has to be Florence, a beautiful city located on the Arno River in northern Italy. The Renaissance started in Italy, partly because of trade. Italy's position on the Mediterranean Sea makes it the major entry point for precious goods being shipped in from Asia and Africa. Wealthy Italian merchants and bankers therefore have plenty of money to spend on art, books, music, and impressive houses. Italy was also the home of ancient Rome, which is an inspiration to Renaissance writers and artists.

FABULOUS FLORENCE

Florence has built its great wealth on its production of fine wool and other fabrics and on its powerful banking industry. At the center of Florence is the huge *duomo* (cathedral), with its amazing egg-shaped *cupola* (dome).

This is the famous dome on Florence's stunning cathedral.

DON'T FORGET THE DAY TRIPS!

Of course, there is more to the Renaissance than just Florence, so this guide has information on other places to visit. These include the Italian city of Venice, gateway to the East; London, England, home of Shakespeare and Henry VIII; and Spain and Portugal, where explorers set sail for unknown lands.

MEET THE MEDICIS

In the second half of the 1400s, the Medicis are Florence's richest and most powerful family. Giovanni di Bicci de' Medici made his fortune from banking in the early 1400s, setting up banks all over Europe and making the Medicis very rich. His son, Cosimo, rose to power in Florence in the 1430s, after plotting against the powerful Albizzi family. From the 1470s to the 1490s, Cosimo's grandson Lorenzo is in charge. Known as Lorenzo the Magnificent, he loves beauty, paintings, poetry, and science, and is a great patron, investing lots of money in art and science projects. He also controls Florence by being friendly with all the top politicians. Lorenzo de' Medici is shown here in an Italian wall painting dated around 1460.

This view of Siena, near Florence, shows the typical surroundings of Renaissance city dwellers.

CHAPTER 2

EVERYDAY LIFE

Everyday life in the Renaissance can be a lot of fun, especially if you have money. You can try on new clothes that have just arrived from abroad, sample exotic foods at dinner parties, test out the latest inventions, and join in the gossip about famous families. But watch what you say, and be careful not to offend anyone. You do not want to end up being poisoned by a jealous rival or being accused of witchcraft. This chapter will help you fit in by choosing the right outfit, polishing your manners, and understanding the ins and outs of Renaissance society.

WHAT TO WEAR

In Florence you will have no problem finding yourself a glamorous outfit. In addition to **importing** all types of beautiful cloth from foreign lands, the city has its own wool industry and is famous for its fine fabrics and fashions. This guide shows you some typical clothes from the late 1400s.

FASHION FOR MEN AND BOYS

A well-dressed Florentine merchant, artist, or scientist usually wears a **doublet** (a snug-fitting vest or jacket) or a flowing tunic belted at the waist. Underneath is a loose shirt, along with **hose** (tight-fitting leggings) and soft leather shoes. The hose may be striped or patterned. Over the top goes a cloak, which can be long or short, and a soft cloth hat, often decorated with a brooch or feather. Hair is worn shoulder length, and you should be clean shaven.

POULAINES

Since medieval times, pointy-toed shoes called poulaines have been popular in Europe. As the Renaissance goes on, they get longer and longer. In the 1400s they are so long that governments have started making laws against them. At their longest, poulaine points measure a ridiculous 24 inches (60 centimeters)—as long as three large bananas in a row! They have to be stuffed with moss to make them stay straight and are attached to the wearer's knees with little chains to keep them up.

FASHION FOR WOMEN AND GIRLS

A wealthy lady will wear a long, full dress made of silk, wool, or velvet, sometimes with a cap, bonnet, or hair decoration. Dresses are often complex and colorful, made from many pieces sewn together. They may be patterned or adorned with silk flowers or embroidery. There is an endless choice of jewelry, cosmetics to whiten your teeth and add color to your lips and cheeks, and products to lighten, curl, and style your hair.

This painting shows a typical Renaissance lady's dress and hairstyle.

WORKING WARDROBES

Working people, such as farmers, builders, bakers, and **artisans**, wear similar clothes: belted tunics, leggings, and long dresses. But they are much plainer and made of undyed cloth.

FASHION VICTIMS

People have always liked nice clothes, but fashion truly takes off in the Renaissance. This is when it becomes important to have the best and latest clothes as a sign of your wealth and **status**.

IN THEIR OWN WORDS

"How oddly he is suited! I think he bought his doublet in Italy, his round hose in France, his bonnet in Germany, and his behavior everywhere."

[A wealthy Italian lady, Portia, describes an Englishman's untidy outfit in William Shakespeare's play *The Merchant of Venice*.]

FOOD AND DRINK

Florence sets the fashion in food as well as clothes. The city even has one of the first-ever cooking schools, called the Compagna del Paiolo, where they experiment with modern inventions such as jelly. Get yourself invited to a wealthy family's dinner party and sample some delicious Renaissance dishes.

GRAND BANQUETS

If you go to dinner in a wealthy household, the host will try to amaze you and the other guests with the latest, most expensive delicacies. There may be several different types of meat, such as lamb, pigeon, venison (deer), or even roast swan or peacock. They will be served with sauces containing precious spices (such as cloves, nutmeg, and saffron) imported from the Moluccas, in present-day Indonesia. Pasta is only eaten by the rich, since it is much more expensive than bread. In a very modern home, you might even get to eat with a fork. However, many people think forks are strange and prefer using a spoon or knife—or their hands.

TABLE MANNERS

To fit in with your fellow diners, here is a handy guide to table manners:

- You will be given a napkin for wiping your hands and mouth, but it is also acceptable to use the tablecloth.
- Do not pick or fiddle with your ears at the table—that is very rude.
- It is polite to share food with your neighbors—but NOT after you have taken a bite.
- After nibbling the meat off a bone, do not put the bone back on the plate! Put it on the floor.

EVERYDAY MEALS

In poorer households food is pretty simple. It is normally beef and vegetable stew or soup, with bread to dip into it. In the 15th and 16th centuries, most people cannot afford dental treatment, and it is normal to have several teeth missing. Dipping your bread into stew or soup makes it easier to chew.

PLATINA

Platina (1421–1481), also known as Bartolomeo dei Sacchi, was an Italian writer born near Mantua. After serving as a soldier, he became an author and wrote many books. One of them was the first cookbook.

Here is Platina's recipe for stuffed eggs. You could try making them yourself.

Boil six eggs for 10 minutes. Remove the eggshells, cut the eggs in half, and carefully remove the yolks. Put two yolks aside and mix the other four yolks with some raisins, grated cheese, chopped parsley, mint, and marjoram. Use the mixture to fill the six egg whites. Then, mix the last two yolks with raisins, a cup of grape juice, and a pinch of ginger and cinnamon. Blend the mixture to make a sauce. Serve the stuffed eggs with the sauce poured over them.

Like the rich, poor people drink wine or wine mixed with water. Most people grow grapes in their gardens and make their own wine every year.

In this painting of a kitchen from the 1500s, you can see lots of kitchen equipment, busy servants, and all types of birds waiting to be cooked.

HOUSES AND HOMES

There is a huge range of Renaissance homes. The poorest families live in simple huts in the country or share a single rented room in the city. Wealthier people rent a whole suite of rooms, and the richest of all have their own grand mansions or palaces.

These painted walls show the members of a typical wealthy household around 1470, including a lord and lady, their children, their servants, and their pets.

Some houses and huts are made of wood, but city buildings are usually built of stone covered with plaster. This does not catch fire as easily, so it is safer for crowded areas. There is no running water or electricity. Water is collected from the local well, and open fires and oil lamps provide heat and light. You will find that even the grandest homes can be quite cold, dark, smelly, and smoky.

FURNITURE

Renaissance dwellings do not have much furniture—just a few basics, such as a table with benches or stools, chests for storing things, and a bed. The bed is the most important item. Often the whole family sleeps there, and sometimes servants, too! From the 1490s onward four-poster beds are popular, with cloth curtains that keep the warmth in. People also hide their money, swords, and important papers in or under the bed.

Most furniture is wooden, heavy, and clumsy, but the rich are starting to want more beautiful versions—such as carved, decorated beds and chests or stuffed, upholstered easy chairs.

This is the room in France where Leonardo da Vinci (see page 24) spent the last three years of his life. It contains furniture from the late 1400s. ➔

RELIGION AND BELIEFS

For a long time the Catholic Church, led by the **pope**, has been very powerful. But during the Renaissance, some writers, scientists, and thinkers are starting to question the church's teachings.

CHURCH WORRIES

Most people in Renaissance Italy are Catholics. They go to church regularly and pray to their favorite saints. But people are starting to worry that some bishops, priests, monks, and nuns are **corrupt**. They ignore their duties and enjoy a lavish lifestyle. Bishops and priests are not allowed to get married. They are not supposed to have relationships with women, but some of them do. Questioning the church can be dangerous, because those who deny its teachings or criticize its leaders may be tortured or put to death. Yet some brave people are starting to do so.

In 1517 a German priest, Martin Luther, attacked the Catholic Church, listing all the ways in which he thought it was wrong and should change. This eventually led to the **Reformation**—the development of a new type of Christianity called **Protestantism**. This process of change is long and painful. During the Renaissance there are many arguments among different types of Christians.

COPERNICUS AND GALILEO

Nicolaus Copernicus (1473–1543) was a Polish astronomer. Around 1510–1520 he developed the theory that Earth and other planets moved around the Sun. The church, however, was not happy with this because the church taught, following various passages in the Bible, that Earth stayed still while everything else moved around it. After Copernicus's death, an Italian scientist, Galileo Galilei (1564–1642), continued his work. Many in the Catholic Church were furious and forced Galileo, under threat of death, to declare that Copernicus's ideas were wrong after all. Another Italian, Giordano Bruno (1548–1600), was burned to death for following Copernicus's teachings.

HUMANISM AND SCIENCE

Humanism is at the heart of the Renaissance. It values the achievements of humans in this world and places less importance on obeying the church in order to be rewarded in heaven. The humanist movement inspires scientists to search for scientific answers to questions about how the world works, instead of simply accepting religious explanations.

SUPERNATURAL BELIEFS

Although they are usually Christians, almost everyone in Renaissance times believes in many other things, too. People believe in **astrology**, which is based on the idea that the stars affect events in everyday life. They also believe in **alchemy**. Alchemists try to turn cheap materials such as lead into precious gold by using special tricks and recipes—although they never succeed. And many people, especially in northern Europe, are genuinely scared of witches. If you are accused of being a witch, you can be hanged, burned, or drowned. However, this is less common in Italy, where people are happy to visit the local *strega* (a type of witch or wise woman) for advice and magic spells to help them solve their problems.

This Renaissance painting, called *The Witches' Sabbath*, shows witches casting spells. However, they do not have black hats or ugly faces—they look like normal women. In the Renaissance, people believed anyone could secretly be a witch.

GOVERNMENT AND POLITICS

In Renaissance times, Florence is not just a city. It is an independent state. It is like a small country, made up of the city of Florence and the countryside and smaller towns that surround it. Most of Italy and other parts of Europe are divided into similar little territories called city-states.

IN THEIR OWN WORDS

"It is better to be feared than loved, if you cannot be both."

[From *The Prince*, a book by the Renaissance politician Niccolo Machiavelli (1469–1527), in which he describes how a ruler should hold on to power.]

ALL-POWERFUL KINGS

In Renaissance times most city-states, as well as larger countries, are ruled by kings, queens, princes, dukes, or other all-powerful leaders. Their power is handed down through families. Sometimes leaders win their power in battles or by invading another state. Once they have control, their word becomes law.

THE REPUBLIC OF FLORENCE

Florence is a **republic**, which means its leaders are voted into power. Every two months the people elect a nine-member Signoria (ruling council) to run Florence. But this is not really **democracy**.

The Signoria, in the Piazza della Signoria, was the center of government in Renaissance Florence.

This painting from 1474 shows a high-ranking government official in the Italian city of Siena. Two clerks can be seen on either side, keeping records. ➜

Only wealthy, male Florentines can vote—not women, servants, or the poor. The real power lies in the hands of Florence's great families, such as the Albizzis and the Medicis. They use their money and contacts to control the Signoria, and they are constantly feuding with each other.

THE COURT OF SULEIMAN

If you want to see a truly powerful ruler in action, visit the eastern city of Constantinople (in what is now Turkey). Here, you will find the court of Suleiman the Magnificent, sultan (king) of the Ottoman Empire from 1520 to 1566. Suleiman gets his nickname because of his incredible wealth, luxurious lifestyle, and great military power.

NEW INVENTIONS

The Renaissance is a very exciting time to visit if you like new technology. Inventors across Europe are coming up with all types of home improvements and handy gadgets. And rich, fashionable city dwellers, in places such as Florence, Venice, London, and Paris (in France), are the first to get their hands on the latest inventions.

CHANGING EVERYDAY LIFE

A modern Renaissance home might feature **innovations** such as clear glass windows, developed in Venice around 1400. It might also have wallpaper, introduced in the early 1500s as a cheaper replacement for **tapestry** wall hangings. There will probably be some printed books, too, after the invention of the printing press in the 1430s. To read the books you might need a pair of eyeglasses, which were invented in Italy at the dawn of the Renaissance, in about 1280.

LEONARDO DA VINCI

Leonardo da Vinci (1452–1519) is probably the most important Renaissance figure of all. In addition to being a great artist, architect, and thinker, he is behind dozens of brilliant invention ideas—although he mostly just sketches them in his notebooks, rather than building them. They include a design for a helicopter, a parachute, a tank, and a machine gun. For part of his career, da Vinci is based in Florence. You can find him there from 1469 to 1481, from 1503 to 1506, and from 1507 to 1508. He once famously said: "There is no higher or lower knowledge, but one only, flowing out of experimentation."

This is a drawing from one of Lenardo da Vinci's sketchbooks, showing a design for a helicopter-like flying machine.

RENAISSANCE INVENTIONS

These are some of the key inventions of the Renaissance:

- Eyeglasses: Around 1280
- Clear window glass: 1400
- Handgun: Around 1430
- Printing press: 1430s
- Pencil: Around 1500
- Pocket watch: Around 1509
- Wallpaper: Around 1510
- Thermometer: 1593
- Self-contained flushing toilet: 1594
- Telescope: 1608
- Parachute: 1617
- Submarine: 1620

This historical illustration shows Faust Vrancic testing his invention, an early parachute, in 1617.

OUT AND ABOUT

The Renaissance is an age of exploration, and there are many inventions to help travelers. Dutchman Hans Lippershey invents the telescope in 1608, and Peter Henlein from Germany makes the first watches in the early 1500s. In 1617 Croatian Faust Vrancic tests the first parachute, and in 1620 Dutchman Cornelius Drebbel invents the first working submarine. It is made of leather and wood, with oars sticking out through sealed holes. It completes a successful test run in the Thames River, in London, at a depth of 15 feet (4.5 meters).

Modern Venetians love to wear masks during the famous Venice Carnival (see page 34), just as they have done for centuries.

CHAPTER 3

THINGS TO SEE AND DO

The Renaissance is the great age of culture, when some of the most brilliant artists, musicians, composers, writers, and architects who ever lived are at work, especially in Italy. This is your chance to see famous paintings, sculptures, plays, and beautiful buildings. However, if you get bored with high culture, there is no shortage of games, street entertainments, cafés, shops, and markets. Even if you stayed in Florence for your whole trip, there would be plenty to see and do. But it is a good idea to visit other parts of Europe, too, to take in some famous sights and experiences.

ART AND ARCHITECTURE

During the Renaissance, artists and architects flock to great cities such as Florence, London, and Paris to work for kings, **aristocrats**, and wealthy merchants.

BUILDINGS

In Florence you cannot miss the stunning cathedral (*duomo*) with its enormous dome. The cathedral had no dome at all for years. Then, in 1420, an architect named Filippo Brunelleschi won a competition to design a new dome. His egg-shaped design (see page 10), completed in 1436, is typical of a new style in architecture. Other great Renaissance buildings include the Louvre in Paris and St. Peter's Basilica in Rome. Renaissance architects like to use the "golden ratio" (a rectangle 1.62 times longer than it is wide) in their buildings. This mathematical proportion was first studied in ancient Greece.

Renaissance style, shown here in the Louvre, in Paris, features columns inspired by the buildings of ancient Greece and Rome.

ART

Renaissance art is also undergoing a revolution. Artists such as Jan van Eyck, from Flanders, Leonardo da Vinci (see page 24), and Hans Holbein, from Germany, are painting with a new attention to detail. They attempt to make realistic portrayals of people and things. They often include modern scientific instruments in their paintings, reflecting the great Renaissance interest in science and discovery.

Hans Holbein's painting *The Ambassadors* shows two French ambassadors to the court of the English king Henry VIII. In the foreground is a strange stretched skull, which can only be seen clearly if you view the painting from a particular angle.

➔

PATRONAGE

Patronage means paying an artist, architect, composer, writer, or scientist for his or her work. Many wealthy monarchs, aristocrats, and merchants are great patrons. For example, a powerful politician such as the Florentine Lorenzo de' Medici might pay his favorite artist to paint his portrait or have an architect build a new public building as a gift to his city. A wealthy Italian lady, such as Isabella d'Este, might pay for a piece of music to be played at her wedding or invite a writer to stay at her court and receive a salary. Patronage is very important because it allows creative people to do their work without worrying about money.

SOME FAMOUS RENAISSANCE PAINTINGS

Make sure you see the amazing masterpieces on this list:
- Jan van Eyck, *Portrait of Giovanni Arnolfini and His Wife*, painted in 1434
- Hans Holbein, *The Ambassadors*, painted in 1533
- Leonardo da Vinci, *Mona Lisa*, painted around 1503–1506
- Raphael, *Saint George and the Dragon*, painted around 1505–1506
- Caravaggio, *David with the Head of Goliath*, painted around 1610

THE THEATER

If you visit the theater in Renaissance Italy, you could see a **commedia dell'arte** show (a type of improvised acting with lots of rude jokes and slapstick humor) or an early opera (another Italian Renaissance invention). But it would be a shame to miss the work of the greatest **playwright** ever: English Renaissance writer William Shakespeare. So, switch your time machine to London in 1600, and see one of his plays at the Globe Theater.

WILLIAM SHAKESPEARE'S GLOBE

In 1600 Shakespeare is working in London with his theater company, the Lord Chamberlain's Men. A year earlier, in 1599, they built their own theater, the Globe, on the south bank of the Thames River. In 1600 you can see a play there most days during the summer. The theater is a tall, circular structure, with three galleries of seats curving around a large, raised stage.

In the late 20th century, a replica of Shakespeare's Globe Theater was built in London. Here, you can see the inside of it, with the seats for the spectators.

SHAKESPEARE

William Shakespeare (1564–1616) was born in Stratford-upon-Avon, an English country town. He married and had a family there, but moved to London in the late 1580s to work in the theater. He was an actor and theater manager as well as a playwright. During his career he wrote more than 30 plays.

SEEING A PLAY

Plays at the Globe are shown in the afternoon while it is still light, since there is no artificial lighting. It costs a penny to watch the play from a standing position on the flat yard in front of the stage. Here, you will find the poorer, rowdier theatergoers, known as "groundlings." To join the wealthy Londoners in the galleries, where you will be protected from the rain, you will have to pay two pennies or more.

In Renaissance times the theater is not a hushed, polite experience—it is bustling, noisy, and messy. Anyone can come in, including children, beggars, and criminals, as long as they pay their penny. You can buy snacks and drinks from stallholders and even throw them at the actors if you do not like their performance. People come and go, talk with each other, or shout rude remarks at the performers.

WHAT'S SHOWING

In the early 1600s, the latest plays to see by Shakespeare include *Hamlet*, the story of a prince who must avenge his murdered father; *Julius Caesar*, about the death of a great Roman emperor; and *As You Like It*, a romantic comedy set in a forest. Renaissance theater comes in several forms:

- Comedies are usually about love, with clowns, jesters, and silly plots involving coincidences and mix-ups.
- Satires make fun of politicians or other people of the time.
- Tragedies often deal with the downfall and death of a king or leader.
- History plays tell true stories about famous people from the past.

MUSIC

Music, and dancing to music, is a huge part of everyday life in the Renaissance. Choirs still sing in church, as they have done for centuries, but people also play music on the streets, in taverns, at parties and celebrations, and in public performances. Renaissance Italy produces many great composers, and almost everyone learns to play an instrument, to sing, or to dance.

This is a selection of Renaissance instruments, painted in 1554. Many of them resemble modern instruments, but are slightly different.

MUSIC FOR FUN

To hear the popular music of the time, just take a stroll around Florence. Street musicians play **lutes** or pipes to earn a few coins, and groups of friends entertain each other with songs or tunes on the chitarra (an early guitar). Any public show, such as a procession or sporting contest, is accompanied by music and dancing.

LEARN YOUR DANCE MOVES

Italian Renaissance dances are made up of complicated patterns of movements. Here are a few that are easy to learn:

- *Movimento*: Rise up on the beat by lifting yourself up on tiptoe.
- *Doppio*: Take three steps forward, rising higher and higher on your toes as you go. On the fourth beat, drop back down.
- *Saltarello*: Take three steps forward, followed by a hop.
- *Reverenza*: Slide your left foot behind your right, bend both knees, and bow politely to another dancer.

NEW MUSICAL INVENTIONS

Most everyday music is traditional and simple. But Renaissance composers are developing new styles and ideas. The **madrigal** from Italy is a typical example. It is a song composed for several different singers, all singing different parts that interweave in complex patterns. Other Italian composers are creating the first ballets and operas by combining music with storytelling on stage. Meanwhile, new instruments are being invented. The first modern violins appear in about 1530, and opera composers use adapted hunting horns in their orchestras, creating the French horn.

Finely dressed ladies, gentlemen, and children dance at a ball in Venice in about 1580.

SPORTS, GAMES, AND ENTERTAINMENT

Throughout the year, towns and cities in Italy and the rest of Renaissance Europe hold festivals, processions, celebrations, and sporting contests. In Italy the most important festival is Carnival. It runs from New Year until the start of Lent (a traditional period of fasting in the Christian calendar, leading up to Easter). During Carnival actors put on plays and people roam the streets playing tricks on each other. Part of Carnival is the **masquerade**. Disguise yourself with a mask to join in the fun, throwing eggs or rotten apples at other revelers.

SPORTS AND RACES

Competitive sports are an important part of Carnival and other festivals. In Rome, donkeys, buffaloes, and old men are forced to race through the streets while spectators shout and throw mud at them. In Florence and Siena the *Palio*, a bareback horse race through the city, is held in the summer. Other sports include *palla maglia* or "mallet ball" (similar to croquet) and *pallone*, a team game in which you hit a ball with heavy wooden paddles strapped on to your arms.

This is a procession of horses, riders, and festival-goers at the *Palio* festival in Siena, Italy, in the early 1600s.

ANIMALS AS ENTERTAINMENT

On your travels you might be shocked to see entertainments involving cruelty to animals, such as letting a pack of dogs attack a bear or forcing cockerels to fight each other to death. Renaissance people do not see anything wrong with this, since they do not think animals' suffering matters as much as many people in the modern world do. However, they do have pets. People keep songbirds in cages and have beloved pet dogs or household cats for catching mice.

GAMES AND TOYS

If outdoor sports sound a bit too energetic, you can relax indoors, or in a shady park or garden, with a peaceful board game. In many European countries both adults and children play chess, checkers, backgammon, and **nine men's morris**, as well as dice and card games. Being good at games will help you make friends and fit in with society.

This painting from 1555 shows girls playing a game of chess.

CAFÉ CULTURE

Renaissance people love to meet up, talk, and gossip over a drink or a snack at a pub, tavern, café, or food stall. Cities, towns, and even small villages are well supplied with taverns. They are basic drinking-houses where people can have a jug of wine or beer and some hot food, such as stew and bread. People also play cards or dice, dance to music, or just sit around the fire talking or telling stories. Alcoholic drinks such as wine and beer have been popular for centuries, but as the Renaissance goes on there is a choice of several exotic imported drinks, including tea, coffee, and hot chocolate.

This painting from the 1400s shows the inside of an Italian inn. You can see men playing backgammon and nine men's morris.

NEW CAFÉ FASHIONS

During the Renaissance the growth in world trade and exploration (see pages 40–47) means that new foods and drinks from foreign lands are starting to appear. Explorers first bring tea from China to Portugal in the late 1500s, and Dutch traders begin shipping it into Europe in 1610. It is most popular in the Netherlands and England, where people like to serve it in fancy teapots.

At the same time coffee, first grown in Ethiopia in Africa and Yemen in Arabia, is spreading through Europe. Since these drinks are expensive, only the rich can afford them, so they are very fashionable. They are served in exclusive cafés called "coffeehouses" (though coffeehouses serve tea as well). Tea is seen as a tonic (health drink), while the **caffeine** in coffee gets the conversation going.

A TASTE OF CHOCOLATE

Chocolate, made from cocoa beans from the cacao tree, was first used as a drink in ancient times in Central America. By 1521 it has been brought to Spain by Spanish explorers such as Hernán Cortés, who have been invading the Aztec Empire. But the Spanish are keeping chocolate a secret from the rest of Europe, and it will not become widely available until the 1700s. To try it out you will have to take a day trip to the Spanish royal court in Madrid.

RENAISSANCE HOT CHOCOLATE

Throughout the Renaissance, chocolate is a drink, not a solid bar. (Chocolate bars will not be invented until 1847.) To experience hot chocolate as the Renaissance Spanish enjoy it, try this recipe:

In a cup, mix 3 teaspoons of cocoa powder with 3 teaspoons of hot water to make a thick paste. Add half a teaspoon of ground cinnamon, a drop of vanilla essence, a teaspoon of sugar, and a teaspoon of honey. Stir well, then add more hot water bit by bit, stirring as you go, until the cup is full.

SHOPPING

Florence and other great Renaissance cities are rich mainly because of trade. Italy's position in southern Europe makes it an entry point for all types of exciting imports from abroad (such as precious stones, fine fabrics, jewelry, and perfumes), so this is definitely the best place to go shopping!

These pendants are typical of Renaissance jewelry, featuring complex patterns, dangling beads, and tiny pictures. →

SHOPS, STALLS, AND MARKETS

In Florence and other Italian cities, streets often have covered **arcades** along each side, where shopkeepers can display their goods, safe from the weather. Artisans, such as leather-workers and bakers, produce items in their houses, then open a window or doorway and sell them to passersby. Street stalls and wandering peddlers sell hot chestnuts or cakes as snacks.

Cities and towns also have market days, when craftspeople, farmers, and merchants bring their goods to a market square to sell. Here, you will find fruits and vegetables, grains, wood and leather goods, pots and pans, and live animals such as chickens. Do not forget to **barter**—if you do not like the price, you can offer a lower one, or even suggest something else in exchange.

VISIT VENICE

The city of Venice, on Italy's east coast, is the trading capital of Europe. Go there during the Sensa Fair, an amazing shopping festival held in St. Mark's Square every May.

CURRENCY AND COINS

Italian Renaissance money is very complicated. Each city has its own coins, and they keep changing in value. However, in Florence, you might use the following coins:

- *Florin*: This is a valuable gold coin.
- *Lira*: This is a silver coin. There can be between 1 and 4 *lire* in a *florin*.
- *Soldo*: There are 20 *soldi* in a *lira*.
- *Denaro*: There are 12 *denari* in a *soldo*.
- *Quattrino*: This is a coin worth 4 *denari*.

All the Venetian merchants and traders use the Sensa to display the most exotic goods they have shipped in from foreign lands. You can buy **ivory** from Africa, patterned silk and velvet from Japan and India, spices such as cloves and nutmeg from Indonesia, jeweled boxes and perfume bottles, and rare animal furs, gems, and carvings. There are also plenty of products made in Venice itself, such as beautiful colored glass. The Sensa goes on for 15 days and attracts shoppers from all over Europe.

These two beautiful decorated glass goblets were made on Murano, an island near Venice, in about 1475.

IN THEIR OWN WORDS

In 1529 Isabella d'Este, marchioness of Mantua and a famous wealthy Renaissance lady, told her friend Jacopo Malatesta to go shopping for her at the Sensa Fair. She asked him to buy "ten or twelve drinking vessels that are different in style, cups and glasses that have thin white filaments without gold."

This late 15th-century painting shows people traveling in gondolas (long, narrow, flat-bottomed boats) on the Grand Canal, in Venice.

CHAPTER 4

ON THE MOVE

In the Renaissance, travel and transportation are not just about getting from place to place to go shopping, attend church, or visit relatives. Explorers are setting out to discover the world, daring to head for the complete unknown. Some people are not even sure if Earth is round, or if they will fall off the edge if they sail too far. Many people are traveling around Europe, too—trading, sightseeing, going to study at a foreign university, or setting off to become an artist, musician, or architect for one of Europe's great rulers. If you would like to join them, this handy guide tells you how to get around and where you can stay the night.

TRAVEL AND TRANSPORTATION

In Renaissance Italy the main way to get around is to walk. If you are going on a long journey overland, you will probably go on foot, maybe using a mule to carry your bags. For shorter journeys people sometimes use horses and carriages, and for going abroad, there are sailing ships.

↑ In this 16th-century hunting party, a wealthy lady rides in a horse-drawn carriage, while some of the huntsmen go on foot.

FLYING MACHINES

The Renaissance is full of new ideas and inventions, and scientists are turning their attention to a new form of transportation: flying machines. In 1507 a Scottish scientist named John Damian built himself a pair of wings using feathers and leaped off the top of a tower. The wings did not work, and he fell and broke his leg. Meanwhile, Leonardo da Vinci (see page 24) designed several flying machines, though none of them ever actually flew. However, Renaissance ideas laid the foundations for later inventions such as helicopters and gliders.

HORSEPOWER

Horses, and sometimes mules, are used throughout Europe for riding and pulling wagons and carriages. But this happens mainly in the cities. Country roads are muddy and full of holes and boulders. This means that carriages soon get stuck and horses get worn out. Also, horses are expensive to buy and care for. However, in Florence, you might see rich gentlemen and ladies out for a ride in a park or setting off for a party in a horse-drawn carriage.

The other place you will see a horse is alongside a canal. Canals are used to transport goods by horse-drawn **barge**, with the horse walking slowly beside the canal, pulling the barge along.

TRAVEL BY SEA

To visit other parts of Europe, such as London, Spain, or Constantinople (in modern-day Turkey), you will need to go by sea. Since the 12th century, when the **rudder** was invented, sailing ships have mostly replaced oar-driven boats. By the 1500s ships are becoming faster and more efficient. However, there are not many special passenger ships—instead, you pay for your passage on a cargo or merchant ship.

FOOD ON BOARD SHIP

It is well known among travelers that the food on board a ship is horrible. You will get hardtack (a type of dry, rock-hard biscuit), along with smelly, stagnant water and maybe some dried peas. Ship food is usually crawling with weevils (a kind of beetle), and many passengers eat in the dark to avoid looking at it! Wealthy travelers take along their own supply of food for the journey, including cheese, salami, and sugar.

PLACES TO STAY

Journeys on foot or horseback can take days, weeks, or even months, so you will have to find somewhere to sleep overnight along the way. This could be a tavern, inn, monastery, or someone's house.

In this painting from the 1500s, a man dances to entertain his fellow guests at an inn.

INNS AND TAVERNS

You have already heard about taverns (pubs where people go to drink, talk, and play games). Many of them also have bedrooms where travelers can stay for the night. Inns are lodging houses with more rooms, and sometimes stables for horses and mules. Some big cities, such as Venice, have a special area of town that is full of inns and taverns, so it is easy for new arrivals to find a place to stay. Otherwise, you can usually find inns along the main roads leading in and out of a town. Outside towns and cities, inns are usually at major crossroads or bridges and at ports, where travelers wait to board ships.

STAY AT A MONASTERY

Another place you can stay is at a monastery, especially if your journey is a pilgrimage. Monasteries are places where monks live and work. They usually have large gardens where the monks grow food. They may also keep bees for honey and may make wine. Monasteries are ideally suited to taking in guests and often have a special **dormitory** set aside for visitors.

Some inns will provide food; others are so basic that you have to bring your own. In the Renaissance it is common for several people to share the same bedroom and even the same bed. You could end up snuggling down with all kinds of fellow travelers, including criminals such as highway **bandits**. Make sure you keep tight hold of your possessions and have your sword handy!

If you cannot find a lodging house of any kind, just knock on the door of the nearest house or farm and ask for shelter. Many households will happily put up a traveler in their shed or stable.

PILGRIMAGES

A pilgrimage is a journey to a holy shrine or sacred place, which people undertake as part of their religious duty. In Renaissance Europe most people are Christians. They often go on pilgrimages to important sites such as Santiago de Compostela in Spain, said to be the burial place of the Christian saint St. James. The city of Rome, the headquarters of the Catholic Church, is another popular destination for pilgrims.

Pilgrims arrive at a holy shrine after their long journey. Many are praying to be cured of illnesses and disabilities.

EXPLORE THE WORLD

The Renaissance is a great age of exploration, when Europeans discover huge parts of the world they had not even known existed. The most important voyages of exploration depart from Spain and Portugal.

A ROUTE TO THE EAST

The driving force behind Renaissance exploration is trade. Until now, precious goods from eastern Asia, such as silks and spices, have made a long, slow journey to Europe, largely by land. Now, Europeans want to make the journey by sea instead, but first they need to find a route.

The Portuguese have spent much of the 1400s exploring the African coast. Finally, in 1497 Vasco da Gama sails around the southern tip of Africa, opening up a sea route to India and eastern Asia. Meanwhile, other explorers, including Christopher Columbus, are sailing west across the Atlantic Ocean. They think Earth is a big ball, and they plan to reach the East by sailing around it. But no one knows for sure. Some believe that if they sail too far south, the Sun will burn them to a crisp. Others think that Earth is flat, and they could end up sailing right off the edge.

During the Renaissance, Europeans are discovering more about the rest of the world and making world maps like this for the first time. This map was drawn in 1536.

CHRISTOPHER COLUMBUS AND THE SANTA MARIA

Christopher Columbus (c. 1451–1506) was born in Genoa, Italy, and later moved to Portugal, then Spain. An experienced sailor, he spent many years trying to persuade wealthy rulers to pay for him to try to reach the East by sailing west across the Atlantic. Finally, Queen Isabella of Spain agreed to fund him, and he set sail with three ships in 1492. One of these ships was the *Santa Maria* (right). When Columbus found land he was convinced he had sailed around the world and reached Japan or China. In fact, he had discovered the Americas—often known in Renaissance times as the New World.

AROUND THE WORLD IN 1,080 DAYS

Set your time machine to September 20, 1519, and you could join the Portugese explorer Ferdinand Magellan as he sets sail from Spain on the first ever around-the-world trip. It takes almost three years. You will not want to stay for the whole journey, because life on board is miserable. The captains of three of Magellan's five ships turn against him, and local people attack the sailors. While crossing the Pacific Ocean, the men suffer from deadly **scurvy**, caused by a shortage of vitamin C from fresh fruits and vegetables. They have to eat rats and boiled leather to survive. In the Philippines, Captain Magellan himself is killed after getting involved in a local battle. Of a crew of more than 230, only 18 men return home to Spain.

This painting shows both the arrest (in 1534) and the execution (in 1535) of British politician and writer Sir Thomas More, for disagreeing with King Henry VIII.

CHAPTER 5

IF THINGS GO WRONG

Like any sensible traveler, you will need to be careful in order to avoid getting sick or becoming a victim of crime. Dangers are everywhere—mugging, burglary, and even murder are quite common. Deadly diseases such as the Plague and smallpox can wipe out millions. And since antibiotics have not been invented, even minor illnesses and infections can be dangerous. However, legal justice systems and medicine are starting to move into the modern age, at least in large cities such as Florence. So, if you are robbed or attacked, injured or sick, you do have a chance of getting some help.

CRIME AND PUNISHMENT

There is no shortage of crime in Renaissance Italy, so hold on to your bag. And make sure you stay out of trouble yourself, because Renaissance punishments are extremely unpleasant.

OUT AND ABOUT

You are probably most at risk when you are on the move, since bandits and highwaymen lie in wait along the roads to rob passersby. Many innkeepers work with robbers to steal their guests' possessions in the night, and pickpockets are active at markets, fairs, and festivals. Try not to get into a street fight. Most young men carry swords or daggers and will often **duel** to the death if they feel insulted. Rome, one of the most violent Italian cities, has a murder rate higher than 21st-century New York City.

ARE YOU A CRIMINAL?

You will be in big trouble if anyone suspects you might be a witch or a **heretic** (someone who disagrees with the church).

PUNISHMENTS AND TORTURES

- Stocks: For minor crimes you might have your feet or arms locked in the stocks in a public place for a few hours. Passersby can taunt you or pelt you with rotten food, mud, or animal dung.
- Banishment: This means being banned from your city or kingdom.
- Amputations: Sometimes a person's hands, ears, nose, or tongue will be cut off as a punishment.
- Flogging/whipping: Being beaten with a whip or stick, in a public place, is a common punishment.
- Hanging: Being hanged by the neck is the most common method of execution.
- Beheading: Having your head chopped off in public with a sword or an ax is considered a good death, since it is usually quick.
- Being hanged, drawn, and quartered: This terrible punishment, mainly used for treason, involves being hanged until almost dead, then having your guts cut out, before being cut up into four pieces. Kings sometimes use it to get rid of enemies who try to steal their power.

A special court, known as the Holy Inquisition, operates in France, Spain, and Italy to punish anyone who opposes the Catholic Church. As for being a witch, just having a strange wart can be enough to make you a suspect.

LAW, TRIAL, AND PUNISHMENT

In Italy each city has its own police force that can arrest anyone suspected of a crime. The police themselves, though, are often cruel and corrupt. Once a suspect has been arrested, he or she goes to court. There, judges hear the accused and the witnesses tell their stories, then the judges decide on a punishment. Sometimes torture is used to make a suspect confess to a crime. Innocent people can end up being punished, while the real criminals escape.

This is a painting, dated 1545, of lawyers in their office. Lawyers know all about the law, and people pay them to help win court cases.

ILLNESSES AND MEDICINES

If you get sick in Renaissance Italy, you will have a huge choice of treatments. You can go to a doctor, **herbalist**, or healer, depending on which type of treatment you believe in and what you can afford.

DISEASES TO AVOID

The most dangerous diseases are spread by insects. You can catch the Plague from the bites of fleas that live on rats. Malaria comes from mosquito bites, and typhus is caused by a **germ** spread by fleas and body lice. All these diseases are killers.

DOCTORS AND HEALERS

If you are unwell you can pay to see a doctor who has studied medicine at a university. Rich people have doctors. There are also hospitals, such as Florence's Santa Maria Nuova hospital, where doctors care for the poor and the sick. However, for everyday illnesses and injuries, you need a barber-surgeon. Barbers, who cut hair, can sew up wounds, fix broken bones, and pull out rotten teeth. They also do "bloodletting" (cutting the patient's arm and letting out some blood), which is wrongly thought to cure many illnesses.

An apothecary weighs out medicine for a customer in his shop, in a painting from the late 1400s.

For medicines, you can go to an **apothecary** or an herbalist. They mix up traditional remedies using herbs, spices, and minerals. There are also "wise women" (or sometimes men), who make their own secret, supposedly magical potions and cures.

This is a 16th-century book about the medicinal uses of plants. This page shows the herb sage, with an explanation of what it can be used for.

IDEAS ABOUT MEDICINE

In the Renaissance, theories from ancient times are still around, including the mistaken idea that the body contains four "**humors**" (melancholy, blood, phlegm, and choler). Illnesses are thought to happen if you have too much, or too little, of one of these humors. However, scientists are beginning to learn more by studying the body closely. And toward the end of the Renaissance, early microscopes will reveal germs for the first time.

RENAISSANCE REMEDIES

Here are a few treatments recommended for common ailments:

- Skin rash: Rub with dock-leaf juice mixed with vinegar.
- Bad dreams: Drink tea made with the roots of the hydrangea plant.
- Scrofula (a skin disease): This is thought to be cured by the touch of a king.
- Baldness: Rub the scalp with burned pigeon droppings.
- Common cold: Put chopped turnip up your nose.
- Headache: Put a tin pot on your head and pour molten (melted) lead into it.
- Chilblains (skin damage caused by cold weather): Rub with a hot mouse skin.

This late 15th-century painted panel, showing St. John the Divine, is by Sandro Botticelli, one of the most famous Italian Renaissance artists.

CHAPTER 6

USEFUL INFORMATION

Keep this useful facts and figures section handy at all times. You can use it to check up on leading artists, writers, scientists, politicians, and other famous Renaissance faces. You can also see at a glance what happened when during the Renaissance—and find out what happened next.

WHO'S WHO?

Here is a quick guide to some of the most famous rulers and artists of Renaissance times.

The Borgias: The Italian Borgia family was famously ruthless. Cesare Borgia (c. 1475–1507) was the son of Pope Alexander VI and became the leader of the pope's armies. His sister Lucrezia (1480–1519) was a great patron who supported several famous artists. She was married three times by the age of 18 (her brother Cesare had her third husband murdered), then finally married Alfonso d'Este, and became duchess of Ferrara in 1501.

Filippo Brunelleschi (1377–1446): Brunelleschi was an Italian architect and artist who designed the famous egg-shaped dome of Florence's cathedral (completed in 1436). He based his style on ancient Roman buildings and influenced other Renaissance architects to do the same.

Isabella d'Este (1474–1539): A member of the wealthy Italian d'Este family, Isabella married the marquess of Mantua in 1590 and became a marchioness. She ruled Mantua when her husband was away at war and used her money to make it a great center of art, literature, and music.

Henry the Navigator (1394–1460): Henry was a Portuguese prince who organized and paid for explorations along the African coast. He hoped to find a trade route to the East. It was finally discovered in 1497, after Henry's death.

Queen Isabella I of Spain (1451–1504): Queen of Castile (part of Spain) from 1474, Isabella married King Ferdinand II of Aragon, uniting the two kingdoms. Together they ruled most of Spain. At this time Spanish explorers were opening up new trade routes and bringing home gold from the newly discovered Americas.

The Medicis: The Medicis were Florence's richest and most powerful family. Giovanni de' Medici (1360–1429) made his fortune from banking in the early 1400s. His son, Cosimo (1389–1464), rose to power in Florence in the 1430s. From the 1470s to the 1490s, Cosimo's grandson Lorenzo (1449–1492) virtually ruled Florence. Known as Lorenzo the Magnificent, he was a great patron, investing lots of money in art and science.

Michelangelo Buonarroti (1475–1564): This Italian sculptor, painter, and architect was considered the greatest artist of his time. He is famous for painting the ceiling and wall of the Sistine Chapel in Rome, designing the dome of St. Peter's Basilica, and creating amazing larger-than-life sculptures such as *David*.

The Tudors: The Tudors were an English family that included several monarchs. King Henry VIII (1491–1547) ruled England from 1509 to 1547. Henry was greatly influenced by the Italian Renaissance and spent huge sums of money on art, music, and architecture.

SOME RENAISSANCE FESTIVALS

These festivals took place throughout Europe, except for those located in particular places in Italy (see list below).

Date	Name	What happens?
January 6	Epiphany	Processions, music, and feasting
New Year–Lent	Carnival	Parties, dancing, dressing up, and playing tricks throughout Italy
March or April	Holy Week	Religious pageants and plays
March or April	Easter	Church services and feasting
May 1	May Day	Dancing in the streets
May	Sensa Fair	Shopping festival in Venice
June 24	St. John's Day	*Palio* horse race in Florence

WHAT HAPPENED TO THE RENAISSANCE?

The Renaissance did not have a definite start or end point, and it reached its peak at different times in different places. It spread around Europe, starting in Italy, then spreading to western and northern Europe.

PROBLEMS FOR ITALY

The Renaissance in Italy was at its peak in the late 1400s and early 1500s. Yet it was already beginning to decline. Lorenzo de' Medici presided over a "golden age" (high point) of art, architecture, and science in Florence until his death in 1492. In the mid-1490s an Italian preacher named Savonarola began to attack the church and also attacked the fashions, luxuries, and artistic creativity of the time, saying they were ungodly. At around the same time, a series of wars started, as other European countries began invading Italy. Renaissance artists, writers, and scientists were still working, but war made life much harder for them.

EUROPE AND THE WORLD

Meanwhile, explorers from many European countries, especially Portugal, Spain, and England, were discovering new foreign lands and trade routes. They found ways to travel all over the world by sea. This meant that goods no longer needed to travel overland across the Middle East, then sail up the Mediterranean Sea to reach Europe. Ships could set out from port cities such as Lisbon (in Portugal) and London, and these cities grew and became much richer, allowing the Renaissance to flower there. The Italian port of Venice, and Italy as a whole, became less important to the rest of Europe.

As Italy became less welcoming to them, some Italian artists and scientists moved to other European countries to continue their work. Leonardo da Vinci, for example, moved to France in 1516.

After 1527, when German armies destroyed much of Rome, French rulers invited a series of Italian artists to France to decorate a great country house, the Chateau de Fontainebleau. From there, Italian Renaissance ideas spread to the rest of Europe.

THE ENLIGHTENMENT

The Renaissance in Europe as a whole is usually said to have ended in the 1650s. It did not end suddenly, but gradually evolved into another era, now known as the Enlightenment. During the Renaissance, science had made great advances. Scientists such as da Vinci, Copernicus, Galileo, and Vesalius had shown the importance of close observation and careful study. Yet the Renaissance was also a superstitious time, when people still believed in witches, magic, and alchemy. Meanwhile, traditional religious beliefs came into conflict with the work of scientists such as Galileo.

During the Enlightenment, science became more important. There was a great emphasis on **empiricism**—meaning that our understanding of the world should be based on what can be observed, measured, and proved. The emotional, artistic, and creative side of the Renaissance took a back seat, while the Enlightenment carried the world toward the modern age.

RENAISSANCE ERAS

Historians often give different periods during the Renaissance different names:

- The "early Renaissance" refers to the beginnings and growth of the Renaissance in Italy, from the late 1300s to the late 1400s.
- The "High Renaissance" is the peak of the Renaissance in Italy, in the years just before and after 1500.
- The "late Renaissance" means the Renaissance from about 1530 onward, after its heyday in Italy was over.
- The "Northern Renaissance" means the Renaissance beyond Italy, especially in countries such as France, Germany, England, and the Netherlands.

THE RENAISSANCE AT A GLANCE

TIMELINE

1304 CE	Francesco Petrarch, "father of the Renaissance," born near Florence.
1346–1351	Black Death (Plague) epidemic in northern Europe.
1374	Death of Petrarch.
1397	Giovanni di Bicci de' Medici heads the Medici Bank.
Around 1420	Henry the Navigator begins funding exploration of the coast of Africa.
1434–1464	Cosimo de' Medici controls Florence.
1452	Leonardo da Vinci—artist, scientist, and inventor—born near Florence.
1453	Constantinople is taken over by the Ottoman Empire.
1450s	First printing of the Gutenberg Bible on Gutenberg's printing press.
1455–1485	Wars of the Roses (civil wars in England).
1469–1492	Lorenzo de' Medici controls Florence and becomes a patron of the arts.
1474–1504	Reign of Queen Isabella I in Spain.
1475	Michelangelo Buonarroti, artist, born near Florence.
1478	Spanish rulers Isabella and Ferdinand set up the Holy Inquisition.
1492	Christopher Columbus discovers the Americas.
1494	France invades Italy, and the Medici family loses power.
1494–1498	Girolamo Savonarola in control of Florence.
1497	Vasco da Gama sails around the southern tip of Africa.
1501–1504	Michelangelo carves his sculpture *David*.
1503–1506	Leonardo da Vinci paints the *Mona Lisa*.
1507	Martin Waldseemüller publishes a new world map.
1509–1547	Reign of King Henry VIII in England.
1513	Machiavelli writes *The Prince*.
1517	Martin Luther challenges the Catholic Church.
1519	Hernán Cortés invades the Aztec Empire.
1519	Ferdinand Magellan sets sail on the first around-the-world journey.

1520–1566	Suleiman the Magnificent rules the Ottoman Empire.
1527	The Sack of Rome—Rome is invaded by German and Spanish armies.
1533	Henry VIII of England breaks with the Catholic Church by divorcing his first wife.
1533	Hans Holbein paints *The Ambassadors*.
1543	Copernicus publishes his theory that Earth moves around the Sun.
1558–1603	Reign of Queen Elizabeth I in England.
1564	Galileo Galilei, astronomer and inventor, is born in Italy.
1564	William Shakespeare, playwright, is born in England.
1608	Hans Lippershey invents the telescope.
1615	St. Peter's Basilica in Rome is completed.
1629–1631	Plague epidemic in Italy.
1633	Galileo is put on trial in Rome for supporting Copernicus.

FURTHER READING

BOOKS

Cole, Alison. *Eyewitness: Renaissance*. New York: Dorling Kindersley, 2000.

Langley, Andrew. *Da Vinci and His Times*. New York: Dorling Kindersley, 2006.

Quigley, Mary. *Understanding People in the Past: The Renaissance*. Chicago: Heinemann Library, 2003.

WEBSITES

- www.twingroves.district96.k12.il.us/Renaissance/ GeneralFiles/RenLinksGen.html
  This website has links to sites all about everyday life in the Renaissance.

- www.learner.org/exhibits/renaissance/florence.html
  This site offers information on daily life, politics, and art in Renaissance Florence.

- www.mos.org/sln/Leonardo/
  This is a multimedia site on Leonardo da Vinci.

GLOSSARY

alchemy blend of magic and chemistry based on trying to make gold out of cheaper materials such as lead

apothecary old word for someone who mixes and sells medicines

arcade covered passage, especially one with shops or stalls on one or both sides

aristocrat member of the ruling or upper classes of a society

artisan craftsperson

astrology study of the positions of the planets and stars, and the belief that they affect events in everyday life

bandit robber or outlaw, especially one who roams country roads

barge long, narrow boat used for carrying cargo along canals

barter argue about the price of goods that are on sale at a market

bribe use rewards to persuade someone to do something for you

caffeine drug found in coffee that keeps people awake and makes them feel lively and talkative

classical name for the cultures of ancient Greece and Rome

close-stool chair with a pot built into it, used as a toilet

commedia dell'arte Italian form of theater involving cartoonish characters, silly jokes, and humorous violence

corrupt immoral and dishonest, especially used to describe those who are supposed to be well behaved, such as judges or politicians

democracy system of running a country or city in which members of the public vote leaders into power

dormitory big room for lots of people to sleep in

doublet type of close-fitting vest or jacket

duel fight, usually with swords, in order to settle an argument

empiricism view that knowledge can only come from scientific study, observation, and experience

germ tiny living thing, such as a virus, that can cause diseases

herbalist someone who makes medicines using plants

heretic someone who disagrees with or argues against a set of beliefs, especially religious teachings

hose tight-fitting leggings

humanism system of thought that focuses on human feelings and ideas, rather than religious ideas or obedience to leaders

humor one of four substances believed to circulate in the body: blood, phlegm, choler, and melancholy

import bring goods into a country to be sold

innovation new invention or idea

ivory smooth, off-white material made from elephants' tusks

latrine pit in the ground that is used as a public toilet

lute stringed instrument that is slightly smaller than a guitar

madrigal song with several interweaving parts

masquerade celebration in which people wear masks as a disguise

medieval relating to medieval times, from about 500 to 1400 CE

nine men's morris ancient game in which players take turns placing stones on a board, trying to make horizontal or vertical lines of three stones in a row

patron someone who pays an artist or scientist to work for them

playwright someone who writes plays (*wright* means "maker")

pope leader of the Catholic Church

privy old name for a toilet

Protestantism branch of Christianity that developed during the Renaissance

Reformation process of challenging the Catholic Church and developing Protestantism

republic state or country that has no monarch and elects its leaders

rudder part of a boat that enables the crew to steer

scurvy disease caused by a lack of vitamin C

status person's standing or position in society

stocks type of locking clamp used to imprison people

tapestry picture made by weaving colored threads into fabric

INDEX

alchemy 21, 59
apothecaries 52, 53
architects 24, 27, 28, 29, 41, 56, 57
architecture 28–29, 57, 58
art 7, 8, 10, 28–29, 57, 58
artisans 15, 38
artists 7, 8, 10, 14, 24, 27, 28, 29, 41, 54, 55, 58, 60

bandits 45, 50
banks 10, 11, 57, 60
books 8, 10, 17, 24
Borgias, the 56
buildings 9, 11, 18, 23, 28

cafés 27, 36–37
Catholic Church 20, 45, 50–51, 58, 60, 61
chocolate 36, 37
clothes 13, 14, 15, 16
Columbus, Christopher 9, 46, 47, 60
composers 27, 29, 32, 33
Copernicus, Nicolaus 9, 20, 59, 61
corruption 20, 51
crime 49, 50–51

dancing 32, 33, 36, 44, 57
da Vinci, Leonardo 7, 9, 19, 24, 28, 29, 42, 43, 58, 59, 60, 61
diseases 49, 52, 53

entertainment 34–35
exploration 37, 46–47, 56, 60
explorers 7, 11, 37, 41, 56, 58

farmers 15, 38
fashion 7, 8, 14–15, 16, 58
Florence 5, 9, 10, 11, 12, 14, 16, 22, 23, 24, 27, 28, 32, 34, 38, 39, 43, 49, 56, 57, 58, 60
food and drink 13, 16–17, 36, 37, 43, 44, 45

Galileo 20, 59, 61
games 27, 35, 36
Globe Theater 4, 30, 31
government 14, 22–23

Henry VIII 9, 11, 29, 48, 57, 60, 61
herbalists 52, 53
horses 34, 42, 43, 44, 57
houses 10, 18–19, 44
humanism 9, 21

inns 44–45
inventions 8, 13, 16, 19, 24–25, 33, 42
inventors 7, 24, 60, 61

London 4, 11, 24, 25, 28, 30, 43, 58
Luther, Martin 20, 60

markets 27, 38
medicine 49, 52–53
Medicis, the 11, 23, 57, 60
merchants 10, 14, 28, 29, 38, 39
Michelangelo 7, 9, 57, 60
money 13, 19, 23, 56, 57
murders 49, 50, 56
music 7, 10, 23, 29, 32–33, 36, 56, 57

Paris 4, 24, 28
patrons 11, 29, 56, 57, 60
pilgrimages 44, 45
Plague (Black Death) 9, 49, 52, 60, 61
poisoning 13, 23
politicians 11, 29, 31, 48, 55
printing press 8, 9, 24, 60
Protestantism 20

Reformation, the 20
religion 9, 20–21, 59

science 11, 28, 57, 58, 59
scientists 7, 14, 20, 21, 29, 42, 55, 58, 59, 60
Shakespeare, William 7, 9, 11, 15, 30, 31, 61
ships 43, 44, 47, 58
shopping 38–39, 57
Sistine Chapel 9, 57
sports and races 34

taverns 36, 44
theater 30–31
thinkers 9, 20, 24
toilets 19
trade 8, 10, 11, 37, 38, 46, 56, 58
transportation 41, 42–43
Tudors, the 57

universities 9, 41, 52

Venice 5, 6, 11, 26, 33, 38–39, 40, 44, 57, 58

witches 13, 50–51, 59
writers 8, 9, 10, 17, 20, 21, 27, 29, 48, 55, 58